Homework
Without Hassles

LARRY KOENIG, PhD

Edited by NYDIA KOENIG, BS, RN

Smart Family Press
3837 Plaza Tower Drive, Suite B
Baton Rouge, LA 70816

800-208-0807
225-293-8170
225-293-5970 fax
www.smartdiscipline.com

ISBN 0-9678023-6-9

Table of Contents

INTRODUCTION

As a parent, my children's success in school is extremely important. If I am honest about it, part of the reason is because their level of success reflects on me as a parent. Our society seems to equate good grades with good parenting and bad grades with bad parenting.

As illogical as this may be, the reasoning is pervasive. Just remember for a moment the last report card one of your children brought home. If it was good, you most likely felt pride. If it was bad (in your eyes), did you feel disappointed? How about guilty? And did you wonder what *you* were doing wrong? If so, did you resolve to do whatever it took to get those grades up? If so, welcome to the crowd.

Perhaps it's as it should be. When it comes down to it, our children need for us to care deeply about their success in school. Children whose parents care loads about success in school certainly have a better chance of also caring. Unfortunately, just caring isn't always enough. Sometimes well intended parental caring can result in constant hassles over school and homework. It depends a lot on the child's attitude toward school.

Typically, there are three ways children approach school work. First, there are those who take to it like ducks to water. They love school work and can't get enough of it. They can't wait until summer is over so they can get back to school. Lucky are the parents who have such children. They can look forward to years of good report cards and (by inference) high marks as parents.

Next, are those children who view school and school work as a necessary evil. They do it because they have to. Usually they would rather be doing something more fun. But then there are also times when they find their homework interesting and they really "get into it." Depending on whether they are either bored or interested determines how much prodding they will need to get their work done. The less often they are interested, the more often homework hassles are likely to occur.

Thirdly, there are those who hate school. They will do anything and everything to avoid schoolwork. Parents of these children usually spend years hassling over school and homework. Some, for the sake of peace, eventually give in and give up. When that happens, everyone loses.

Good news! Effective strategies exist to turn the tide. Attitudes over homework and school can be changed. Homework hassles can be halted. And children can be motivated to do their best work on their own.

Toward this end, this book is devoted. It is my hope that you can use this book to help your children develop a love for learning and a belief that says "I have what it takes to be successful in school (and in life)." That's the bottom line.

CHAPTER ONE

Why Homework is Important

I think it's important to know just why homework is important for two reasons. First, so we can over a period of time, get our kids to understand it's importance. The idea is this. Over a period of time children (believe it or not) pick up on and adopt their parent's attitude that homework is a top priority. Secondly, we as parents need to be clear on it's value to do what our children need for us to do. This we especially need when our children are doggedly determined to fight us every step of the way. At these times we need every reason we can find to fight the urge to give in or give up.

So let's look at the reasons why homework is so important. Some are more obvious than others.

Reason #1

Positive Belief Formation: There is a direct relationship between self-esteem and success in school. The more a child adopts the high self-esteem belief that he "has what it takes to be successful in school" the better he will do. Or, conversely, the more a child adopts the negative attitude that he "doesn't have what it takes to be successful in school" the worse he will do. Over the last 25 years there have been numerous studies which bear out this correlation. As parents we know it is correct, intuitively.

Homework plays an important role in the development of these beliefs. This is because of the constant feedback a child gets about himself in relation to homework.

What I mean is this. Children adopt beliefs about themselves by listening for information about themselves. They listen to parents, relatives, teachers, and friends. When they hear something about themselves, they make a conclusion and look around for other evidence to determine if it is true or not. If they find it, the child starts to repeat the belief over and over again in his "self-talk" until it becomes a solid belief. Once a solid belief, he acts it out consistently and automatically.

Let me give you an example. When I was in the second grade, one of my favorite things to do was to draw. One Tuesday afternoon, my teacher said we were going to have art class. She asked us to take out our papers and crayons and to draw anything we liked. I chose to draw some hills behind my house. It was a winter scene with snow, a deer on one side and a rabbit on the other. I thought it was a masterpiece. Secretly I hoped the teacher would come by and say something nice about it.

Sure enough, just as I was putting the finishing touches on it, the teacher stopped at my desk and picked up my drawing. I was smiling from ear to ear. But then she said to the rest of the class, "Look at Larry's picture. He's still drawing baby pictures."

Step one was accomplished. I had some information about myself. With all the bravery I could muster, I choked back the tears. On to step two, I looked at my lollipop trees and concluded the teacher was right. My conclusion was "I can't draw". Step three was accomplished when future opportunities to draw came up, I picked out imperfections and again concluded that I couldn't draw. After awhile it became a belief which I consistently acted according to.

Children adopt beliefs about themselves over their abilities to handle school work in the same manner. The daily and most frequent feedback they get is in relation to homework.

Parents see it. Teachers see it. Everyone evaluates it and makes comments to the child. Out of these comments, the child makes conclusions which boil down to either "I have what it takes to be successful in this subject," or the reverse.

Once the feedback is given and the conclusions made, the child looks for further evidence to support his conclusions. As he is seeking, he will usually find the evidence and end up adopting the conclusion as a belief.

If enough positive beliefs are established, the child further concludes "I have what it takes to be successful in school." This is, by-the-way, the same child who tends to love school and school work.

On the other hand, if enough negative beliefs surrounding school work are established, the child further concludes "I don't have what it takes to be successful in school." These, of course, are the ones who buck against school, teachers, and homework all the way.

In summary, homework is important because of the daily feedback which it draws to the child. If done correctly, neatly, and on time all kinds of positive comments are made which lead to positive productive beliefs. If done incorrectly, sloppily, or not at all, the reverse happens.

Please note: *Further chapters will reveal how to motivate your children to do homework correctly, neatly, and on time.*

Reason #2

Grades: Time spent doing homework directly affects grades. In fact you can almost predict the grades on your child's report card by the grades on his homework. The two usually coincide.

In fact, teachers will tell you that a child at any level of academic achievement can improve his grades by concentrating on homework. With great certainty, educators can tell parents that students who consistently do homework out perform those who do not.

This is why I tell parents frustrated over poor report cards to stop harping over grades and change their focus to homework. Doing so can give both the parents and the child a handle on a solution. More on how to do this later.

Reason #3

Responsibility and Accountability: Lucky is the child who has a parent who conveys the message that he is responsible for doing his homework. And further shall be held accountable for it being done correctly, neatly, and on-time.

Does this sound old-fashioned? If it does, I defend it on the basis that I believe a child growing up shouldering responsibility and accountability has a better chance at being successful in all aspects of life. Spiritually, emotionally, and mentally he will do better. A child brought up in such away, I assure you, will fare a whole lot better in his career and relationships too.

Knowing most of my readers are educated, successful people, I look to you for proof of this. I ask you—*did your parents hold you responsible and accountable for your homework?* You bet they did. And our kids need us to do the same for them.

Reason #4

Self-confidence: Through doing homework a child learns "how to gain knowledge." As they learn from independently doing their homework they start to establish a belief that says "I have what it takes to learn."

This is a powerful belief. One which can lead a person to great achievements in life. It gives a person a sense of competence with which to succeed in life.

If you have this sense about yourself that "you have what it takes to learn", let me ask you a few questions. How did you get this belief? Can you relate it back to school and homework? How has it helped you in life? I rest my case.

Reason #5

Persistence: Who was it that said, "More in life is accomplished through persistence than anything else?" Whoever it was, succinctly put into words what all successful people eventually find out. That is, persistence pays off. As my Dad always liked to say, "Honest effort is never lost."

Parents can deliver this lesson through homework. Children needing to learn the value of persistence will provide you with ample opportunities for you to encourage them to persist. Sometimes they will even need you to insist that they persist.

As I talk to successful people, so often they give credit to their parents for their "you can do it" messages and encouragement to stick with it in spite of the struggle.

Keep in mind, homework is supposed to be hard. Kids are meant to struggle over it. And struggle is a good thing, not a bad thing that they need to be spared from. Through struggles over homework persistence can be taught.

Reason #6

Time Management: Couldn't we all use a good course in time management? Especially in how to overcome procrastination. Let me speak for myself. I know I sure could benefit from one.

It is quite evident that many of today's young people could benefit from learning how to budget their time too. I know this from the surveys I take from my audiences across the country. Parents consistently report their children either not doing their homework until the last minute or even not getting it done at all.

The antidote? You guessed it: Homework. In the following chapters I'll discuss just how you can get your children motivated to do their homework on their own and in a timely fashion. Along the way, you may even be able to teach your kids the valuable lesson of how to postpone pleasure. Or, as our parents put it, "Work comes before play."

CHAPTER TWO

Three Rules Children Need Parents to Insist Upon

Before we get started into this chapter, let me first acknowledge that some kids do not need these rules. These are those delightful kids who love school work, breeze right through it, and are likely to work ahead in their book. All these kids need is your support and encouragement.

For the rest, the three rules in this chapter will go a long way towards:

A) Preventing and eliminating homework hassles

B) Motivating "best of ability" quality

C) Motivating "timely" completion

D) Motivating independent work.

These rules will take care of the majority of what you need to do as a parent in relation to homework. Specific problems and solutions will be dealt with in Chapter Four.

I titled this chapter "Three Rules Children Need Parents to Insist Upon" for a good reason. It is because by insisting that these rules be followed, parents can help insure that their children get the most out of the homework experience. That is:

✏ High self-esteem

✏ Good grades

✏ Responsibility and accountability

✏ Self-confidence

✏ Persistence

✏ Time Management Skills.

I mention the benefits again because the rules, though simple in theory, take time, patience, and diligence to implement. When you think about it, this makes sense.

What I mean is this. No way can we expect our kids to accrue all of these, great benefits without ourselves putting in a good measure of effort. As our parents have told us time and again, "There ain't no such thing as a free lunch!"

So get ready. Here we go.

RULE #1

Establish a Time For Homework

As parents we can either help our children set up a consistent time to do homework or leave it up to them to do it when they feel like it.

Hmmmm. Let's see now. What choice shall we make?

If you buy into the idea that homework is important and you want to communicate this to your children, there is only one choice; to establish "Homework Time." The very act of doing so says "Homework is top priority at our house."

How much time?

On average an elementary student may need up to one-half an hour a day. Middle school, thirty to sixty minutes, and high schoolers may need up to an hour or so (some days more for major papers and projects).

Based on the idea that our adult work day is typically eight hours and a child's school day is six hours, these time amounts would seem reasonable. If your child's homework demands a great deal more or less than this, it's time to sit down with the teachers and discuss why. More about this later.

When?

Many kids today either have after school activities, designs on playing when they get home, or face other circumstances which make doing homework after school difficult. However, there are some who both can do it right after school and prefer to do it then.

A good rule of thumb is to set "Homework Time" for as early as possible while allowing for a break after school. For some families, early as possible may mean 4 p.m. while for others it may mean 6 or 7 p.m.

To determine the time, I suggest having a family meeting to discuss the matter. As adults do, children more willingly comply with decisions in which they participate. Three guidelines should be followed in making the decision:

1. Make the same time each day if at all possible. This is the best way to establish a habit.

2. Make it so the completion time will be no later than 7 p.m. for elementary children, 8 p.m. for middle schoolers, and 9 p.m. for high schoolers. When you think about it, is homework likely to get done neatly and correctly after these times? Probably not. Besides, all of us, kids alike, need time for rest and relaxation.

3. All other activities such as phone calls and television should be postponed until "Homework Time" is over.

One can expect that after establishing "Homework Time," a few problems will emerge. These will include such things as:

■ Dragging out the task

■ Procrastination

■ Deal making

■ No homework

■ Lost assignments

■ Books left at school

■ Miscellaneous creative excuses.

We will deal with these "challenges" in Chapter Three. Suffice to say here that establishing "Homework Time" will be easier decided upon than carried out. It will take time, patience, and persistence on your part. But it will be worth it. Problems will be prevented and successful life skills taught because of your efforts.

RULE #2

Establish a Homework Place

As our mothers taught us, "There is a time and place for everything." And the place for homework is not the kitchen table, on the phone, or in front of the television. Common sense dictates that these places are not conducive to learning. Neither do they give homework a place of importance.

The "Homework Place" should be one of privacy. A place where your child goes to during "Homework Time."

Ideally, it will be a place where your child can work privately without distraction from other people. And it will be stocked with whatever items he needs to complete his homework. For the most part this means writing paper, pencils, pens, and a pencil sharpener. Special projects, of course, demand other items. These can be supplied on an "as needed" basis.

The whole idea of establishing a "Homework Place" is to help your child identify homework as a major responsibility. Therefore, it has a special time and place to be accomplished.

In the same family meeting where you establish the time, you can discuss the place you. Once you and your children have agreed upon their Homework Time and place, you are ready to discuss the third rule with them.

RULE #3

Homework is to be Done Alone

1. To explain this rule, go over the following points:

2. Homework is a child's responsibility

3. You will answer questions when you can, but the child must complete the work

4. You will occasionally check homework to see if it is done correctly and neatly.

This is very similar to the way that parents of "baby boomers" approached homework. That's interesting because "baby boomers" tend to do the opposite with their kids. That is, many of these parents play a major role in the completion of homework.

This, unfortunately, leads to problems. For one thing parents over-active with homework run the danger of robbing their child of the homework values mentioned earlier; high self-esteem, good grades, responsibility, self-confidence, persistence, and time management skills.

No parent wants to do this. But that's just what happens when a parent shoulders the responsibility for homework and studying. While not intending it, this parent is giving his child the message "you don't have what it takes to be successful in school without my help."

Sometimes well intending parents get trapped into doing just this. It happens when they want to make sure their child does well in school. Their way of making sure is by hovering over them and supervising their studies.

This, I admit, is tempting to do sometimes. Especially when a child is struggling. But it is just such a time when our children need us to insist that they do their homework on their own.

To insist on Rule #3, you will be giving your children the message that they have what it takes to be successful in school. Some children, especially those addicted to "parental help", will resist this message. They will argue in every way they can that they need their parent's help.

This is understandable. They are afraid. But what they really need is a parent willing to say, "Yes, I understand it is hard, but homework is your responsibility and you can do it if you stick with it." Lucky is the child who has a parent willing to give this message.

Off in the future, I can hear some of you saying, "But you don't understand. My child really does need my help in order to pass." This is a very real issue for some and I'll deal with it in the next chapter. For now...

- Establish the rules

- Expect some dissent

- Remember the benefits

- Insist the rules be followed

CHAPTER THREE

15 Common Homework Problems (And Uncommon Solutions)

Let's dive right into the problems and see what we can get done. The sooner the better. Homework problems, left unresolved, can destroy the peace of a family and a child's future.

Too many times I have heard from families who spend their evenings anguishing and arguing over homework. So often the kids in these families decide they don't have what it takes to be successful in school. When this happens, it frees up 100% of their time to disrupt their families and their schools. Twenty-five percent of the kids in America make this decision and drop out of school. It's tragic. And it's time to take action! So let's take a look at some of the common problems and some uncommon solutions.

PROBLEM #1

"I Don't Have Any Homework"

Sometimes it's true. Other times trusting parents are shocked to hear it was a lie. They usually find out too late. After they look into poor report cards they find out the reason was because homework wasn't handed in.

How is a parent to know? "Trust but verify" is my answer.

Example:

Dad: Do you have any homework tonight?

12-year-old son: Nope.

Dad: I've been hearing that a lot lately. How come?

Son: I do mine at school. The teachers give us time.

Dad: That's great son. For the next few weeks I want you to bring it home so I can look at it.

Son: Awe, Dad, that's stupid!

Dad: Negative comments aren't necessary. What is necessary is for you to show me your work.

Son: Oh, all right, if I have to.

The idea is this. Every child gets some schoolwork to do almost every day. As I mentioned before, some kids love it and do it willingly. Others avoid it out of frustration, disinterest, or hate.

Those who avoid homework need parents willing to check up on their homework. Besides looking at schoolwork papers, it is wise to at least check with the teacher(s) and ask two questions:

1. Is my child handing in his homework on time?

2. Is it handed in neatly and correctly?

Once you start checking up on homework, you won't hear "I don't have any homework" near so often. That brings up the question, though, of what to do with "Homework Time" when there is no homework.

Some family psychologists and educators suggest that the time be filled with some form of schoolwork anyway. I would say it depends on the circumstances. If grades are good and homework has been up to snuff, why worry about it. Let your child enjoy his night off from homework in the same way your parents did with you.

If, however, homework and grades have been suffering, the homework time should be filled with schoolwork, which can strengthen apparent weaknesses.

To identify weaknesses and practice work, which will help, confer with your child's teacher. If you show an interest, so will she. And most probably she'll have some other great suggestions too.

PROBLEM #2

"It's too hard"

If your child is complaining that his homework is too hard, one of several possibilities exists.

Most often a parent can interpret this statement to mean, "I don't know how to do my homework." So the first solution is to go over the instructions with your child. After doing so, be sure to send him back to do the work on his own.

Another possibility behind his "Too Hard" complaint is that he is seeking some attention and sympathy. This isn't unusual either. All of us human beings like some loving attention when we are doing something difficult.

The thing not to do here is to try to convince him that it's not hard. This will only cause him to prove to you that it's too hard by not being able to do it.

A better tactic is to respond with something like:

Daughter: "This math is too hard for me."

Mother: "Yes, algebra can be tough to understand, can't it?"

Daughter: "Yeah, especially factoring equations."

Mother: "I can remember having trouble with that, too."

Daughter: 'Well, I guess I better go get started on it."

By letting your child know it's ok to feel the way she is feeling, you allow the child to:

1. Feel good about herself

2. Feel good about you

3. Let go of her feeling.

"Too hard" can also mean that the work is beyond your child's present level of comprehension and ability. Indicators that this might be the case include:

1. Consistent inability to do assignments correctly

2. Failing marks on homework and tests

3. Consistent expression of frustration from your child over the subject matter.

If this is the case, the problem most likely will not resolve itself. However, the temptation that many parents face at this point, which should be resisted, is to "help the child with the homework." Oh, sure, it is ok to help some. But it is not helpful to sit with the child night after night and help him do his assignments.

The reason this is not helpful is that the teacher needs to know if your child can't do the work. You need to know too. The sooner the better for your child.

When the indicators mentioned before present themselves it is time to meet with the teacher and to ask for his or her help. Most teachers are more than happy to go out of their way to assist a parent seeking help.

When you meet with the teacher, attempt to:

1. Identify the problem.

2. Agree on a plan of action.

3. Set up ways and times to determine if the problem is getting resolved.

Follow through is the cost important thing at this point. Also important is changing whatever isn't working and trying different things.

In seeking solutions, don't forget to ask your child what he thinks would help. I know of one mother who tried this tactic with her seven-year-old son who couldn't read. Every conventional method had been tried and failed.

When asked, he suggested comic books. Mom and Dad said ok and let him pick some out. Several weeks later he was not only reading, but it was one of his favorite things to do.

PROBLEM #3

"I'll do it later."

I wonder how many kids in America put off their homework until the last possible minute. According to the informal surveys that I take from parents at my "Up With Parents" workshop, it's a bunch. Dragging homework out causes a couple of major problems. First of all, families end up fighting and bickering about it all night. Then, when it is done "later" it gets done quickly and sloppily.

The solution lies in the insistence on "Homework Time" as described in **Chapter Two** under **Rule #1**. If procrastination is a problem this rule needs to be enforced as consistently as possible.

Also, it is a big help to suspend all other privileges once homework time starts. You will want to let your children know what these things are. Your list might include things like:

1. Telephone calls

2. Television

3. Friends over

4. Video games

5. Going outside.

In fact, by suspending all privileges until, homework is done, you can motivate your children to not drag homework out all night. This can work like a charm but you have to watch for the following:

· Quite often children will plead to use the phone because they either need to get the assignment or some help from a friend. To counteract this let your kids know all phone calls will have to be made and completed before homework time starts.

· Some children, in order to get to watch a favorite TV show or to get on the phone will scurry through homework. The results are often less than satisfactory.

If this becomes a problem with your kids, let them know that privileges don't start until homework is completed and checked for neatness and accuracy.

· Also we need to watch out for ourselves. By our very nature, **we** parents tend to be inconsistent. We will strictly adhere to our rules, one day and not the next. We can prevent loads of homework hassles by setting the rules and consistently enforcing them.

PROBLEM #4

"Will you help me?"

When, as a parent, we are faced with a request from our child for help; our natural response is to help. Giving assistance to our children is part of our job as parents. It not only helps them, but it makes us feel useful to boot.

In relation to homework, a little help is just fine. It should be limited to helping a child understand instructions or helping with a couple sample problems. The child should then be sent back to his "Homework Place" to complete the work. Doing so gives the message, "You are competent to do your school work." To give more help than this can lead to problems. Some kids get addicted to help. Or rather they get attached to the attention and become "attention addicts."

If you have ever been around an attention addict, you know what a problem it is. This child is always at your side pleading for your attention. Send him away and he'll be back in a blink of an eye.

A child addicted to homework help will argue convincingly that he cannot possibly do his homework without your help. Many parents give into it without realizing that each time they:

1. Reinforce the child's need for help

2. Reinforce the child's belief that he "doesn't have what it takes to do his school work on his own."

So, here's the Catch-22, we want to help our children with their homework when they ask but we don't want to get them addicted to being helped.

The solution is in Rule #3: Homework Is To Be Done Alone. The more a child resists complying with this rule, the more he needs you to insist upon it. Because of your insistence, he will eventually learn that he is competent to learn on his own. How wonderful! "Yes, but," someone usually replies, "you don't understand." "If I don't help my child, he will flunk."

My response is this. If your child can't do the work on his own, he should flunk. Big red F's in the education process are not all bad. They signify that something is the matter and something should be done about it. Helping a child pass can circumvent this process.

What I mean is this. Let's say that your eight-year-old son has a reading problem. So, you work with him every night in his workbook making sure all of his homework is done correctly. You do such a good job that the teacher doesn't catch the problem and your son passes on to the Fourth grade. Now your son has a major problem because he is in the Fourth grade with Second grade reading skills.

To avoid this problem, help a little and insist he do the rest on his own. If he can't, make an appointment to meet with the teacher as discussed in the section on **"It's too hard."**

PROBLEM #5

"It's still not perfect."

Kids shed so many tears because they can't do something "just right." For these perfectionist children, it's all or nothing. Either it's perfect or it's worthless. What do we parents do with this? With the best intentions we say things like:

"Oh, Jennifer, you shouldn't feel that way. Look how nice your drawing looks. I love it!"

Or...

"You shouldn't be so hard on yourself, Clint. You got third place. That's not bad at all for someone only fifteen."

As parents we say things like this both hoping to give our kids a healthier perspective on themselves and to spare them from emotional pain. If your child is a perfectionist it won't work. The more you reason one way, the more he'll reason the opposite.

To assist your perfectionist to achieve a healthier point of view, try either clarifying the feelings or identifying with your child. For example:

"Jennifer, it seems like you are real disappointed in your drawing. Is that right?"

Or...

"I can remember a time when I lost a race, too. It was a regional cross-country race in which I could have qualified to go to the state championships. But I lost. What a disappointment."

Such responses are much more likely to meet with positive responses than the ones, which contain words "you shouldn't." These words tune out and turn off kids and adults alike.

In the extreme case, if you have a child who is constantly whining that whatever it is, isn't right, you may assert something like, "It is ok to want things to be done right. And it is ok to feel bad if it isn't the way you want it. It is not, however, ok to whine or cry about it. If you want, we can talk about it and you can try to correct what you don't like. But, no crying or whining allowed".

PROBLEM #6

"What's the matter? It's ok to me!"

For every perfectionist child in the world, I think there are ten who gloss over their mistakes without a thought. Although this attitude toward homework can be frustrating to parents, research indicates non-perfectionists get more accomplished.

Unfortunately for these kids, grades are given on quality, not quantity. Homework needs to be done correctly and neatly in order to assist a child to develop the values mentioned earlier. Remember?

· High self-esteem   · Self-confidence

· Good grades   · Persistence

· Responsibility   · Time management

Homework done sloppily just won't "get it". If this is a problem for your child, try this:

Step One: Check homework on a daily basis. Also check work done at school.

Step Two: If done sloppily, show your child what needs to be corrected. (You may want to point out examples of his work done correctly.)

Step Three: Send him back to do the work over. Do not allow privileges until it is done correctly.

If your children come to know that you won't except homework done poorly, they will start to do it right the first time.

One caution, though, is not to get too picky. Doing so can destroy a child's innate love of learning. If you have questions over homework quality, check with the teacher. She can tell you what her expectations are.

PROBLEM #7

"I'm no good at_____."

When a child says "I'm no good at blank" he may well be saying he:

· Wishes he was good at it

· Needs help

· Believes he can't do it

· Has no interest in it

· Etc., etc., etc.

With so many possibilities, the easiest way to find out is to ask.

10 year-old Mandy: "I'm no good at math."

Dad: "Sounds like you are having trouble in math. Is that right?"

Mandy: "Yeah. I'm just no good at it."

Dad: "I'm wondering what makes you say you are no good at math"

Mandy: I don't understand any of my math homework that's why"

Dad: "So, what do you think would help?"

Mandy: I suppose I could call Cindy. She's good at helping me."

Clarifying feelings and asking for the child's solution works a lot better than taking the temptation to do this:

Mandy: "I'm no good at math."

Dad: "Sure you are, Honey."

Mandy: "No, I'm not."

Dad: "All you need to do is study harder and you'll do fine."

Mandy: "No, I won't."

Dad: "Well, you'd better. Without math you won't be able to go to college. You'll end up on welfare so you'd better just get in there and buckle down."

Mandy: "Well, I can't, so I guess I'll just go on welfare. College isn't important anyway!"

By the time this conversation ends, both Mandy and her dad are likely to be so angry with one another the whole evening will be ruined for both. Lucky is the child whose parent chooses to:

1. Clarify feelings.

2. Brainstorm solutions.

PROBLEM #8

"I've got a major project due."

Consider the following scenario. It used to be common place at our house.

The scene starts as supper is getting over. Our kids, being All-American kids, ask the question so many kids ask after supper.

"Can we turn on the T.V. now?"

Being All-American parents, we would ask in return, "Is your homework done?"

Answering as All-American kids, the response was always something like, "I didn't have any homework," or "I did mine at school," or "I did it on the bus".

Never did we hear them say, "Oh, what was I thinking of? I've got lots of homework tonight."

It just didn't ever happen. So, of course, we would give permission for the TV to be turned on. Some of the kids would watch TV, one would get on the phone, and the rest would go count their zits in the mirror.

About nine o'clock or so, my wife and I would get the kids off to bed and sit down to watch television ourselves. Invariably one of the kids would pop out of their bedroom for a conversation like this:

Jennifer: "Dad, would you help me with my homework, please?"

Me: "I thought you told me you had your homework done. What's the problem?"

Jennifer: "I know, Dad, but I forgot something."

Dad: "What Jennifer? What did you forget?"

Jennifer: "I'm sorry, Dad, but I've got a major project due."

Dad: "When is it due?"

Jennifer: "Tomorrow."

The next three hours would then be spent on a scavenger hunt for that big piece of white cardboard, glue, glitter, and markers. Whatever it took we would get that thing done so she could march into school with it the next day.

This was foolish. It sure didn't teach anything about responsibility or time management. After numerous such incidents we finally changed our methods and have worked out the following plan. It works well and prevents tots of problems.

Step One: Have a family meeting to discuss major school projects.

Step Two: Tell your kids from now on, if assistance or materials will be needed for a project, you are to be informed of the project when it is assigned. Tell them this will be the only time you will be willing to work out the details with them.

Step Three: Work out the details on projects of which you are informed of in a timely fashion. Refuse to assist with projects "forgotten 'til the last minute."

If your kids are All-American kids, they may test you to see if you mean business. The only way to pass this test is by sticking to what you said. This, of course, is tough when you have a child wailing "You don't love me" and "I'm going to get an 'F' and it will be all your fault!"

At such times, your child needs you to insist on sticking to your guns. If you do, she'll learn that you mean what you say. And she will learn to plan ahead for her projects.

PROBLEM #9

"I forgot it at school."

Did you ever notice that forgetting homework at school is never a problem for good students? For some reason these kids always remember their books and homework. No, it's the students having trouble with schoolwork who forget. This is no big problem if it just happens occasionally. But for the repeat offender, a plan of action must be sought. I suggest:

Step One: Buy your child an assignment book.

Step Two: Require that your child fill it out each day. If needed, require that he have the teacher sign it.

Step Three: Let him know that if for any reason he forgets his assignment book or homework, all privileges will be suspended for that evening. Let him know what the privileges are (for example: television, telephone, video games, going outside, friends over, etc.)

If you follow this plan, your child will "forget" one day and protest how "unfair" you are. Most likely he will also have a barrage of both excuses and great reasons why you should give him another chance. Your child, I believe, will be best served if you respond with:

"Yes, you do deserve another chance. You will get it tomorrow. As for today, no privileges."

PROBLEM #10

"Homework is stupid."

Negative attitudes are tough to deal with. I think our kids know it. Some even have an uncanny ability to use them against us. Let me tell you what I mean.

In the normal course of events, we parents nag our kids. We do so to prod them. It's necessary because there isn't a child alive who always does what he is asked the first time. (Unless his parent's use my *Smart Discipline System*. To order, see the last page.)

Unfortunately, as we verbally prod our kids, we are likely to use angry and critical comments. Being smart enough to know not to be directly critical right back, our kids sling back a negative comment sure to send us up the wall. It all goes like this:

Mom: "Jason, it's time to do your homework."

Jason: "I'll do it right after my program is over, OK?"

Mom: "That's what you said an hour ago. I want you to do it right now."

Jason: "C'mon, Mom. Just ten more minutes, OK?"

Mom: "Oh, alright, but then turn off the TV, OK?"

Jason: "No problem."

Mom: (thirty minutes later) "Jason, why are you still watching TV? You never listen to me. What is your problem anyway?"

Jason: "Homework is stupid, that's what."

Mom: "What do you mean homework is stupid?"

Jason: "It just is. And so is school. I'm going to drop out when I'm 16 anyway."

If you have ever witnessed a conversation like this, you know there is no happy ending to it. Conversations like these end up in screaming matches where all sorts of ugly, hurtful comments are made.

Prevention is the best tactic. Trying to reverse the course of the conversation once tempers flare is difficult to do.

Prevention isn't all that easy either. Especially if two people have fallen into a muddy, slippery, foul rut of responding to each other in the way I just described. Changing takes some real effort.

To change, keep in mind that:

"If you change the way you respond to a person, he has to change the way he responds to you."

You can prove this for yourself. Analyze any communication pattern you have with a loved one. Identify what you usually say and the likely responses. Then decide how you can respond differently the next time the pattern presents itself. Your results will be revealing, I'm sure.

If you have a child who makes negative comments about homework and school, try the same thing. For example, the mother in my example might think:

"Most every night I seem to get into an argument with Jason over homework. What happens is usually this. He starts watching TV and doesn't get to his homework. Then I start reminding him. He then puts me off until start nagging him. He then says something negative and I get really angry and yell at him."

At this point, mom might brainstorm some alternative ways of responding, such as,

1. Discussing the problem with Jason, when calm, and asking his ideas for a solution.

2. Letting Jason know that from now on the television will be turned of at 7 p.m. every night and not turned back on until his homework is done.

3. Deciding to talk slowly and quietly in response to inflammatory statements. (This option causes anger in both parties to subside.)

Once alternatives are thought out, one can be selected for use.

It takes some time and effort to go through this process. But it can help break up major negative communication patterns.

Have patience with yourself when you try this process out. Communication patterns are deeply ingrained. They can be changed, though, with effort and persistence.

PROBLEM #11

"I'll do it when you get home."

With so many working moms, lots of children either come home to an empty house or to a sitter after school. By the time mom gets home, it is late with meal preparation and housekeeping chores waiting for her.

Sure would be nice if homework was already done, wouldn't it? Unfortunately, children often stall doing homework until a parent is there to "make them."

If this is a problem at your house, try the following tactic. Give your kids a choice. Tell them they may either have their homework done before you get home or they may wait to do it after you get home. However, if they choose the latter option, tell them there will be no privileges that evening. No television, no phone, no video games, no visits with friends.

Such choices are motivational. They work well and can easily be modified to fit your situation.

If you won't be home until it's too late for homework, insist that completed assignments be laid out for you to see when you get home. Make weekend privileges dependent on their completion.

For instance, let's say your daughter goes to the movies every Friday night. In this case, you tell her homework must be done each evening or no Friday night movie.

Try it. You will be surprised how much better this works than screaming and yelling.

PROBLEM #12

"Homework always takes me all night."

Do you have a child who drags his homework out all night? If so, something should be done for everyone's sanity. Pondering over homework all evening can drive the whole family nuts.

One solution is to suspend all privileges until homework is done. This strategy works like magic for most. Others are unfazed by it. They dawdle all night anyway.

In such a case, insist on a starting and stopping time for homework. When homework time is over, collect the books and papers and put them up. Tell them any homework left undone is between them and their teachers.

This is a great lesson in living. On the job, a person has to learn to get his work done on time. If not, he has to explain why to his boss and face the consequences. The more times it happens, the more severe the consequences.

But consequences are between him and his teacher. You are only there to consult and motivate as needed. And to teach a little time management on the side!

PROBLEM #13

"That's not the way the teacher said."

Isn't it funny. Our kids come to us asking for help. We help them. Then they complain to us that "That's not the way the teacher said to do it." Frustrating, isn't it? For the occasional perpetrator of this complaint, you can usually dispense of the situation by having them explain how the teacher wants it done and then sending them to go do it.

For the constant perpetrator of the complaint, plan ahead. Next time help is sought, ask the following question; "How did your teacher say to do it?" If the response is "I don't know", then ask, "How can you find out?"

Usually your child can find out how to do something from either a friend or the teacher. While often we can give them the help they seek, it can be much more helpful to direct them elsewhere. It teaches self-reliance. And it prevents complaints about the quality of our help.

PROBLEM #14

"Why can't I do it in front of the TV?"

Hmmm. Let me see now. Let me count the reasons:

1. It is virtually impossible to concentrate on TV and on homework at the same time thus quality suffers.

2. Doing homework in front of the TV gives the message that homework is not important.

3. Doing homework in front of the TV drags out the task.

Having reasons "why" you decided on something rarely appeases kids, though. Usually they just cause further arguing.

Sometimes saying, "Because I said so" is the best responses. It cuts off the argument and allows both you and the child to go on to more important things.

While TV distracts from homework, music helps. Music facilitates memory and concentration. It works so well, in fact, that we can remember the words to songs we learned thirty years ago. Sometimes just hearing a song will also bring back memories otherwise forgotten. So next time you insist that television must be off during Homework Time, suggest that they turn on their stereos!

PROBLEM #15

"My teacher's unfair"

Children complain about teachers. They say things like:

"My teacher gave me too much homework."

"My teacher is always picking on me."

"The teacher didn't explain this so I could understand it."

When faced with complaints about teachers, we have several types of responses to choose from. The first two are both common and counterproductive.

One choice is to ask for details about the complaint and then respond with something like "You're right. I'll talk to the teacher and get her straightened out!"

Major harm is done to a child when such comments are made either to or within a child's hearing range. Kids who hear comments that put down teachers learn contempt and disrespect for teachers. When this happens they turn off to learning.

While no parent would intentionally do this, sometimes, adverse things are said in attempts to aid our children. To avoid harming the child's attitude toward learning, it is essential that any and all negative comments about teachers be kept from the ears of children.

Another way parents respond to complaints about teachers is by lecturing to the child, "If you wouldn't waste so much time at school, I bet you could get all your homework done in study hall. I know I used to. The problem is that you're just plain lazy."

Again, parents make comments like this with good intentions. They think that a little good advice coupled with insightful comments about a perceived character flaw will cause a child to change his attitude and behavior. The reverse usually happens though.

Instead, attitudes and behaviors worsen. To prevent this, a third response to teacher complaints is better utilized. In this option, the parent listens and clarifies feelings.

For example:

Jeff (coming in from school): My teacher stinks.

Dad: Sounds like you had a hard day at school.

Jeff: Yeah, well, It wouldn't have been so hard if it wasn't for Mrs. Jensen. She's always on my case for no reason.

Dad: Tell me more.

Jeff: Well this is just one minor example. She told me she was sick and tired of me being late for class and that next time she was going to make me stay after school. That was so unfair. I was only 10 seconds late. And besides she never says anything like that when other kids are late.

Dad: Let me see if I understand. You feel like Mrs. Jensen treats you unfairly and your angry about it, is that right?

Jeff: Yeah, and some days she just really bugs me. Oh well, I guess I can handle her for now. Schools out in three weeks anyway.

In this example, Dad may well have had a huge urge to either come to his son's aid by putting down the teacher or by lecturing and giving advice. But, Jeff was better served when his dad chose to listen and to clarify his feelings. By doing so he gave Jeff the following subconscious messages:

1. I care enough about you to take time to listen to you.

2. It is O.K. to feel the way you feel.

3. You are competent to handle your own problems.

These are powerful and wonderful messages to give a child. They are well worth the effort and time it takes to listen and clarify feelings.